What Do We Know About
Crop Circles?

by Ben Hubbard

illustrated by Andrew Thomson

Penguin Workshop

For Gill and Anthony, parents and skeptics—BH

For Rhia and Cerys—AT

PENGUIN WORKSHOP
An imprint of Penguin Random House LLC, New York

First published in the United States of America by Penguin Workshop,
an imprint of Penguin Random House LLC, New York, 2022

Visit us online at penguinrandomhouse.com.

Library of Congress Cataloging-in-Publication Data is available.

Printed in the United States of America

ISBN 9780593386750 (paperback)   10 9 8 7 6 5 4 3 2 1 WOR
ISBN 9780593386767 (library binding)   10 9 8 7 6 5 4 3 2 1 WOR

Contents

What Do We Know About Crop Circles? . . 1

Early Circles 6

Modern Examples 16

Return of the Thing 28

The Researchers 40

Cereologists and Croppies 53

Bower and Chorley 67

Hoaxing Undercover 79

Hoaxes Revealed 88

Crop Circles Today 98

Timelines 104

Bibliography 106

What Do We Know About Crop Circles?

In 1966, something strange happened on a farm by the town of Tully, near the northeast coast of Australia. At 5:30 a.m., the farmer's dog began barking and then bounded away toward a nearby lagoon (a small lake). Farmer George Pedley drove his tractor to the lagoon later that morning and heard a loud hissing noise. He thought it might be a punctured tire, but suddenly, a large object rose from the lagoon before him. It was gray, the size of a bus, and shaped like a saucer. It spun rapidly as it rose. Then, the object tilted slightly and sped into the sky, faster than a jet plane. The hissing noise disappeared with the object, but a strong smell of sulfur remained.

Pedley ran closer to the lagoon to take a look.

Normally there were high, standing reeds—tall grasses—covering the water's surface. But now, there was a saucer-shaped circle in a spiral pattern on the surface, formed by flattened reeds. The circle measured thirty feet across.

The "Tully Saucer Nest" made headlines across

Australia. Investigating police and scientists said the circle had probably been made by a whirlwind, a column of air moving in a funnel shape. But Pedley disagreed. "I've seen wet whirlwinds and dust whirlwinds. If the police believe this, let them. I know what I saw. It wasn't a whirlwind."

The next day, two more circles appeared on another Tully lagoon. Only a few feet across, the circles were also filled with flattened reeds. Soon, circles were being discovered across south Australia in wheat and barley fields. Some fields had up to twenty circles of different sizes. There were also reports of bright lights and Unidentified Flying Objects (UFOs) around the circles. But scientists could not find any evidence of UFOs.

Of course, it was possible that someone had made the circles during the night—perhaps as a hoax, or trick—but the scientists did not think humans were involved. So who, or what, was creating the circles? Although they would not be called by this name until 1983, the mystery of modern crop circles was born.

CHAPTER 1
Early Circles

People have reported seeing crop circles for hundreds of years. A short booklet from 1678 describes a circle in a field of oats in Hertfordshire, England. Oats, like wheat and barley, are crops that farmers grow and cut down at harvest time in late summer. But in 1678, the farmer could not find someone to cut the oats. He needed a "mower" to harvest them. Although he was rich, the farmer was also miserly. He did not want to pay the wages the mower had asked for. He told the mower that "the devil himself should mow his oats before he should have anything to do with them."

That night, the field of oats appeared to be on fire. The next day, the farmer found that the oats had been cut down in a round, swirling circle. No one could have done so much work in one night, and it frightened the farmer. He explained the circle as the work of a "Mowing Devil" and was too afraid to remove

his crops. *The Mowing Devil* is illustrated with a creepy figure cutting the crops.

It is not the only example of such strange circles in England at this time. Circles of flattened grass, called fairy rings, were also reported. In the Middle Ages, fairies were believed to be creatures with magical powers. Some were thought to look like tiny, winged women and live in the woods and cause mischief. Fairies dancing together in circles were believed to be responsible for the fairy rings of flattened grass.

In 1686, Oxford University professor Robert Plot was asked to investigate the fairy rings. Some of them were up to 150 feet across! Plot said the circles may have been caused by male deer rutting (locking horns) or by moles during mating season. He also thought a whirlwind or a lightning storm may have made the circles. Plot interviewed people who said they saw "hollow tubes of lightning" and "bright balls of light" around the circles. Plot did not solve the mystery.

Crop circles, balls of light, and objects from the sky had also been mentioned in North American legends by the Algonquian people, who were among the first to settle in parts of Canada and the United States. The Algonquian were made up of separate nations, such as the Cree, Cheyenne, and Odawa, who all shared the Algonquian language.

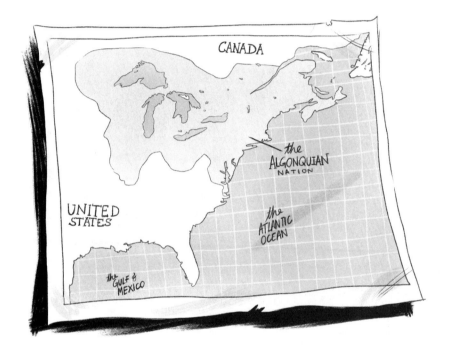

According to an Algonquian legend, a hunter named Algon found a perfect circle of flattened grass in a prairie one day. But there were no footsteps leading to the circle. While Algon wondered how the circle was formed, a basket full of women descended from the sky and landed in the circle. In the middle of the circle was a shining ball that the women danced around. They used sticks to strike at it.

Legends like this one and English folklore provided explanations for crop circles at a time when people didn't have scientific explanations for much of the world around them. Eventually, science was able to provide rational reasons for many things. Crop circles, however, continued to confuse people. Even as reports of new crop circles kept emerging.

In Guildford, England, in 1880, scientist John Rand Capron was out walking after a storm

and found a circle of flattened wheat. The wheat stalks were bent over at the base and formed a spiral pattern. What surprised Capron most was the neat outer edge of the circle. What had made it?

Capron wrote about

John Rand Capron

the circle in a scientific journal called *Nature*. Because it had been found after a storm, he thought a whirlwind might have caused it. Nearly one hundred years later, many new theories about crop circles and whirlwinds were being discussed. And some of them were out of this world.

What's Inside a Crop Circle?

Modern crop circles are usually formed in fields of crop plants such as wheat, barley, canola, oats, peas, corn, mustard, and rye. They appear during the summer months when the plants are fully grown. Inside the circles, the crop stalks are bent over flat just at ground level. At the outer edge of the circle, the plants remain standing.

Crop circles range in size from 3 feet to more than 165 feet across. Often the circles appear along a field's tramlines, or parallel tire ruts. These are small tracks made by the farmer's tractor wheels. Most crop circles appear very suddenly under the cover of night and are discovered the next day. The circles last only until the farmer mows or plows them over.

CHAPTER 2
Modern Examples

During the 1960s, reports of crop circles became more frequent, and not just in Australia. They were also appearing in the United States. Some reports included eyewitness accounts of Unidentified Flying Objects hovering near the crop circles. This led many to believe crop circles were the work of extraterrestrials, beings from another planet.

In Marion County, Oregon, in 1964, ten-year-old farmer's son Michael Bizon said he saw a shiny UFO land in a wheat field. The UFO smelled like gas, made a "beep-beep" noise, and "took off like a rocket." Bizon's father found one large circle of flattened wheat with three smaller circles around it. The local sheriff said the place "where all the wheat was flattened did indeed look suspicious."

The US Air Force investigated. A lieutenant questioned Michael Bizon several times. He reported: "Everyone's story remains the same. The boy's father and mother, the Marion County Sheriff, the carpenter working there . . . they all back the boy up." The cause of the circles, however, was left unsolved.

Other crop circles were reported on American farmland in Montana, Michigan, and Indiana. Eyewitnesses reported strange balls of light rising from the ground and in some cases burning their skin. After flying away, the balls left behind circular patterns in the fields. Investigating scientists said the lights may have been caused by burning paper, marsh gas, or balls of lightning.

But some scientists said the crop circles could be hoaxes—

Marsh gas

circles made by people to trick others into believing they were left by something mysterious, such as aliens. This hoax theory would become a major part of the modern crop circle story.

The mystery continued when twenty-seven new circles were found in a wheat field in Veblen,

South Dakota, in 1965. The local newspaper asked for an expert to explain the circles, as the current theories "ranged from whirlwinds to whirlpools to interplanetary visitors." The air force concluded that whirlwinds had caused the circles. However, a local expert found there was "no logical explanation" for the circles.

Whirlwind

Around the same time, crop circles were also being reported in Canada. Some of these circles were very big. They measured over thirty-two feet across. As with the United States examples, UFOs and balls of light were seen near the crop circles. Other crop circles were reported in Argentina, Brazil, France, Australia, and the Netherlands. However, the largest number came from the country where they were first reported so long ago: England. Here a crop circle appeared in 1966 that made headlines both in England and abroad.

For years, there had been strange sights in the small market town of Warminster, Wiltshire. These included bright lights and fireballs in the sky. Others reported seeing a gray, cigar-shaped UFO with portholes along its side, like a ship.

Arthur Shuttlewood

Then, in 1966, crop circles began appearing. A local newspaper reporter named Arthur Shuttlewood was sent to investigate. He wasn't sure what to call the crop circles and UFO sightings. So he wrote an article describing them as "the Warminster Thing."

Shuttlewood felt certain that alien spaceships were making the crop circles. Some of the circles were in grassy fields, but Shuttlewood also discovered a circle of flattened reeds on a small lake. The reeds spiraled in a clockwise direction

and were almost identical to the "saucer nests" found in Tully, Australia. Amazingly, they were also found only a few days after the Tully nests.

Then, in 1972, Arthur Shuttlewood claimed to have seen a crop circle actually forming right in front of him in a wheat field. "The grain flattened like a lady's fan being opened up. A perfect circle resulted in less than a minute," he wrote. But he had seen nothing that was causing the motion. Shuttlewood kept discovering crop circles throughout the early 1970s, and he even

wrote several books about them. If something unexplained happened in Wiltshire, reporters would call Shuttlewood. However, today it is thought Shuttlewood exaggerated many of his stories. When he stopped reporting on UFOs and crop circles, they stopped appearing. By the mid-1970s, the UFO and crop circle craze had died down in Wiltshire. This, however, would not last.

UFOs and Crop Circles

In the 1960s, UFO sightings increased around the world. This was an exciting period in history when the first people were being sent into space. Russian Yuri Gagarin had become the first man to travel into space, in 1961. In 1969, American astronaut Neil Armstrong became the first man to set foot on the moon.

Humans became fascinated by what we might find in space. Books, comics, movies, and TV shows about UFOs and extraterrestrials became big business. More and more people became convinced they had seen a UFO, especially in remote and rural areas. Eyewitnesses usually said these UFOs were saucer or cigar shaped, and that their round landing pads left behind circular imprints. Some people believed this could explain what the crop circles really were. Others thought the crop

circles were messages left by alien life forms to communicate with people on Earth.

CHAPTER 3
Return of the Thing

In August 1980, there was dramatic news from Wiltshire, England: "Mystery Circles—Return of the 'Thing?'" announced a local newspaper headline. The

article reported that three large crop circles had been discovered in wheat and barley fields below the Westbury White Horse. Tourists visiting the horse were the first to spot the crop circles. Soon, many other visitors arrived to see it for themselves.

Most visitors said the circles were both beautiful and bizarre. Each one measured nearly sixty feet across and had a spiral pattern of flattened stalks within it. The edges of the circles were so neat that some visitors said no human being could have made them. And there were no footprints leading to the circles. Some said that they must have been formed by something from above, such as a UFO or maybe a weather pattern. The farmer said the circles could not have been made by wind or rain. He suggested the blades of a helicopter were to blame. "If it's not a helicopter, then it is very mysterious," he said.

The Westbury White Horse

The White Horse is a giant figure carved into the chalk of Westbury Hill, Wiltshire, England. The horse was created in the late 1600s, probably to remember the Battle of Edington. This was a famous battle in 878 CE, when the Anglo-Saxon king Alfred defeated the invading Vikings.

The Westbury White Horse was recarved in the 1850s to keep its white color visible. In the 1950s, it was painted over in white cement.

Westbury Hill is also the site of an older Bronze Age (3000 BCE–1000 BCE) burial site, as well as an Iron Age (beginning around 1000 BCE) fortress.

Dr. Terence Meaden

One local scientist disagreed with the farmer. Dr. Terence Meaden was a former physics professor who published a journal about tornadoes and strange weather. Meaden had read the newspaper article about the new crop circles and decided to investigate. He concluded that the circles had been made by a whirlwind. A whirlwind is a spinning column of hot air that rises from the ground. Meaden said the spinning would explain why the plant stalks were flattened in a spiral direction. However, such whirlwinds were very rare, he said. They might never occur again.

But the very next week, three more crop circles appeared in the neighboring county of Hampshire. Here hikers had found the circles in a place called Cheesefoot Head. This is a large flat area surrounded by hills that looks like a natural sports stadium. Local newspaper reporters were soon at the scene. The owner of the field was furious, saying that people had made the circles and also damaged his crops. A neighboring farmer disagreed, saying a helicopter was to blame. The circles themselves were between twenty-five and sixty feet across and ran in a line along the crop tramlines. No one was more excited by the circles than Terence Meaden. The circles, he said, were definitely made by whirlwinds (sometimes called dust devils).

The next summer, more circles emerged in Wiltshire and Hampshire. Local shopkeeper Ray Barnes said a circle had occurred right in front of him. Barnes was out walking when he heard a hissing noise from a nearby wheat field. Then an

invisible line appeared to flatten the crop like a cookie cutter. The circle was formed in about four seconds. In 1983, there was another eyewitness account. Melvyn Bell was horseback riding when a whirlwind of dust rose up from a wheat field.

A few seconds later, the wind stopped and the dust began to settle. Below it, a thirty-foot circle had been carved into the crops.

By this time, there was interest from national newspapers and television. Many reporters were eager to talk to Terence Meaden about the circles. After all, he was a scientist, and his whirlwind theory sounded convincing. Meaden was so sure of his theory that he reported that crop circles were "a mystery no longer."

Terence Meaden's Plasma Vortex Theory refers to a whirlwind that forms over a crop field. The theory says that if the air spins fast enough, it creates a bulge at the whirlwind's bottom. This causes the crops to flatten in a spiral pattern. Meaden thought that the air could spin fast enough to become electrically charged and appear as a glowing and humming ball. (When a gas, such as air, becomes electrically charged, it's called plasma.)

But then something happened to challenge Meaden's theory. In late summer 1983, some new crop circles were found at Cheesefoot Head. This time, the circles formed a geometric pattern: four smaller circles surrounding a larger circle in the middle. Because there were five circles, the formation became known as "the quintuplet."

Quintuplet formation

It looked planned out, like a pattern you might draw with a compass in math class. Some said it looked like the four landing feet of a UFO. Others asked: How could a whirlwind make a pattern? Meaden said it was possible. The quintuplet had been formed by one main whirlwind that then came down in four separate places around the outside. Many people believed Meaden, but other people researching crop circles strongly disagreed.

CHAPTER 4
The Researchers

Meaden was not the only Wiltshire local who had become fascinated by crop circles. In 1983, engineer Colin Andrews was driving past Cheesefoot Head when he saw a crowd in the field below. He went to have a look and was amazed by the quintuplet formation there.

Another engineer named Pat Delgado had also recently stumbled upon a crop circle. He said that standing inside a circle had made a sensational impact on him. Delgado and Andrews decided to team up and become crop circle researchers. It was Colin Andrews who first came up with the name "crop circles."

Being a crop circle researcher meant documenting every new crop circle that appeared. Some researchers even documented crop circles around the world. The research kept Delgado and Andrews busy as new circles were popping up nearly every week. As soon as they heard about a new circle, the men would drive to investigate, by taking photographs, making measurements, and checking that the crop stalks were bent and not broken. Soon, they were joined by pilot Busty Taylor, who would take them up for a bird's-eye view.

Delgado and Andrews did not believe the

circles were being made by whirlwinds. "'Plasma vortex' is a technical term invented by Meaden to cover something he doesn't understand," Delgado said. Instead, Delgado and Andrews thought there was a more mysterious cause for the circles.

Delgado thought that "energy force fields" *inside* the Earth were making the circles. This energy would pull at the crops like a giant magnet and bend them over in a spiral pattern. Delgado also believed this energy could be detected using a tool called a dowsing rod. Dowsing rods were often used in the past for finding water beneath the ground. Delgado said that dowsing rods showed high levels of energy inside a crop circle. This energy then disappeared when the person holding the rod stepped outside the circle.

Colin Andrews using a dowsing rod

Dowsing Rods

A dowsing rod is a forked stick or metal rod used to locate underground water. The person with the rod (the dowser) holds two ends of the forked stick in their hands, with the third end facing forward. The dowser then walks slowly over the ground to be tested. If the dowser passes over water, the forked stick is supposed to twitch, or point downward.

Some people say energy fields beneath the ground can also be discovered using dowsing rods. Two bent metal rods will rotate when the dowser walks over the supposed energy. Although dowsing—the art of using dowsing rods—has been used for thousands of years to find water, scientists say there is no proof that the practice works.

Andrews and Delgado were not the only ones who believed crop circles were connected to energy fields. Visitors often reported that strange things happened to their electric equipment while standing inside a circle. Watches and cameras would stop working, and video tapes were erased. They said it felt like there could be a giant magnet just below the circle. One visitor even reported being knocked off his feet.

Andrews and Delgado believed that something was controlling the energy—some sort of "superior intelligence." It might be aliens from space, they said, or something inside the Earth itself. If crop circles were messages from a superior intelligence, the trick would be to figure out what the messages meant. The  circles were often made in patterns of four or five circles, so geometry could be the key.

The crop circles' geometric patterns also explained a larger question about them. Why were the largest number of the world's crop circles appearing in a small section of southern England? The answer, they said, was linked to the area's ancient past. Wiltshire and Hampshire are home to many structures and symbols built by Bronze Age people, including large standing stones, such as Stonehenge.

Stonehenge

Constructed between 3000 and 1520 BCE, Stonehenge is a circle of standing stones built on Salisbury Plain in England. Over eighty large bluestones and sandstones were used in the monument, the largest of which stands thirty-two feet high and weighs forty-five tons. Surrounding the stones is a large ditch and many circular holes.

The holes held the cremated (burned) remains of people. Aside from Stonehenge being a burial site, no one is certain why it was built. Many believe it was created for rituals held by ancient priests. Because some of the stones are aligned to the sun, Stonehenge may have been used to observe the moon and sun and to help determine the farming and planting calendar.

There is another circle of standing stones, constructed at Avebury in Wiltshire, England. At over one thousand feet across, it is the largest Bronze Age stone circle in the world. This circle is also close to many of the crop circles that appeared in the 1980s.

Delgado and Andrews believed the ancient standing stones were connected to crop circles.

They said the same energy fields that created the crop circles were also running beneath the circles of standing stones. Some people call these energy fields ley lines. A ley line was simply a straight track in ancient times that connected two villages or towns.

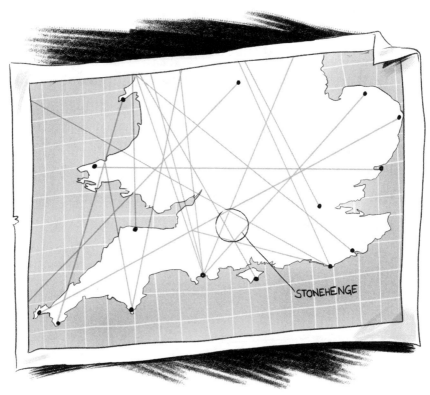

Ley lines in southern England

Andrews and Delgado said the stone circles were built to mark where a ley line was. Crop circles would then appear farther along the ley line. Delgado and Andrews had no scientific proof for their theories, but many crop circle believers took them seriously.

Terence Meaden said that Bronze Age people didn't understand that the crop circles were caused by whirlwinds. Instead, they thought some god or supernatural creature was responsible. They therefore worshipped the circles by copying them in giant circles of standing stone. Although he was a scientist, Meaden did not have any proof for this theory, either.

CHAPTER 5
Cereologists and Croppies

By the late 1980s, southern England had become the crop circle capital of the world. In 1987, over seventy circles were reported; in 1988, there were over one hundred. In 1989, over three hundred circles appeared. The crop circles were not only growing in number, they were also becoming more complicated. There were many

formations with four or five circles, as well as circles with rings around them.

Tourists from all over the world flocked to England to see the crop circles. Many wanted to experience standing in a crop circle for themselves. Suddenly, farmers found groups of visitors trampling over their fields to get to a circle.

Many visitors didn't understand that they should walk along the tramlines to avoid damaging the crops. Farmers put up signs saying there was no access to the circles, but this did not stop the tourists. Clever farmers set up stalls at the entrance to their field and charged people a fee—around two dollars—to enter.

Many visitors reported strong sensations when they entered a circle. Some instantly developed a headache and feelings of nausea. Others said they felt a sense of calm and even entered a trance, or state of bliss. Some people lay down in the center of the circle and meditated or prayed. Some were sure the circles were portals to other worlds. A few tourists said they had visions of mysterious beings watching them. Others drew pictures of the aliens they said had created the circles. Often the aliens had large, oval-shaped heads, with big black eyes, like in movies and comic books.

The believers in a supernatural explanation for the circles became known as "croppies" and "cereologists." Ceres is the name of the ancient Roman goddess of agriculture, and "ology" means the study of something. Being a cereologist became an interesting summer pastime for many people. Cereologists

Statue of Ceres

spent time traveling to new crop circles and meeting other fans and followers.

Several cereologist groups were formed. Circles Phenomenon Research International (CPRI) was the group run by Pat Delgado and Colin

Andrews. For them, crop circles were not a pastime. They were an obsession. Delgado and Andrews had even published a crop circle book in 1989 called *Circular Evidence*. The book became a best seller, and even the queen of England, Elizabeth II, had a copy. In the same year, over three hundred crop circles appeared in Wiltshire and Hampshire. Many were formations of five circles, but one with six circles also appeared. It had been an exciting summer, and there was great anticipation for what the following summer would bring. It would not disappoint.

In April 1990, as crops in England started to reach their highest growth, the first crop circles began appearing. These were small circles at first, but large fifty-five-foot circles were also discovered. Then a completely new type of formation appeared. It had two circles—one forty feet across and the other ten feet across—linked by a rectangle. Four narrow rectangles ran alongside. The rectangles amazed cereologists—no one had ever seen straight lines in a crop circle before.

The formation looked like a picture, so people called it a "pictogram." More pictograms appeared the following week. Then, in July, a pictogram appeared in a wheat field in Alton Barnes, Wiltshire, that surpassed all others. This was a double pictogram, linked by lines, with rings, circles, and key shapes coming off them.

Known as the Eastfield pictogram, this

The Eastfield pictogram, 1990

formation caused a great stir. It was shown around the world in newspapers and on television. Today, it is one of the world's most famous crop circle formations. It has been reproduced in books and was used on an album cover by rock band Led

Zeppelin. Although it was very exciting, the pictogram raised serious questions. How could pictograms be created by whirlwinds? Many people had believed  Terence Meaden's Plasma Vortex Theory. But it was hard to see how spinning wind could create straight lines or patterns.

Meanwhile, Colin Andrews and Pat Delgado had their own theories. They said the new pictograms proved that a superior intelligence was making the crop circles. The intelligence was increasing its attempts to communicate with humans by making more and more complicated formations. To prove this, Andrews and Delgado said they would capture a crop circle being made. This would show the world that crop circles were being created by something more mysterious than wind or humans.

To capture a crop circle being made, a major surveillance operation began on top of the Westbury White Horse hill.

Called "Operation Blackbird," the surveillance was sponsored by the British Broadcasting Corporation (BBC) and Japan's Nippon Television (Nippon TV). The television networks provided high-tech, low-light cameras. The British Army supplied thermal imaging equipment. Volunteers operated the equipment and stood guard overnight.

Stretching out below the hill were gently sloping fields of untouched wheat. The first crop circles of 1980 had been discovered there. Now, Delgado and Andrews felt it was only a matter of time before a new formation would appear.

Two nights later, at 3:30 a.m., the thermal imaging equipment picked up strange orange lights. Something was moving in the wheat fields below the hill. At 5:30 a.m., Colin Andrews began

calling journalists. In a live interview on a BBC morning television show, Andrews reported:

"We do have a major event here. . . . We have two major ground markings, which have appeared in front of all of the surveillance equipment. . . . We have helicopters over the top, to film in detail what we have here, before anyone enters the field."

Andrews then called a 10:00 a.m. press conference on the Westbury White Horse hill. Attending journalists began reporting that "excited scientists said they recorded evidence on Wednesday that could solve the centuries-old mystery of circles in English cornfields."

A large crowd quickly gathered. Andrews, Delgado, and two television producers then walked down to the wheat fields below. Before them were the unmistakable shapes of crop circles. Standing by the edge of the first circle, Delgado said to the cameras: "This is the first time any human has entered these circles." Delgado described the circles as the men walked farther in. Planes and helicopters with cameras flew above. The crowd on the hill waited impatiently for news. Then people noticed something small and blue in the center of each circle. What were these objects? Could they be messages from space?

Delgado and Andrews reached the first of the blue objects. Then they fell silent. Each circle had a cluster of sticks in its center. On top of the sticks was a blue paper board game called Zodiac. The circles were a hoax—an elaborate practical joke! Andrews, Delgado, and the whole world watching had been tricked. The crop circles had not been made by other life forms of superior intelligence, but by humans.

CHAPTER 6
Bower and Chorley

Watching Operation Blackbird with great interest were two local men in their sixties—Doug Bower and Dave Chorley. They were crop circle hoaxers. For over thirteen years, Bower and Chorley had been making the circles across southern England in the dead of night.

Doug Bower and Dave Chorley

After laying down a circle, the pair would go to their separate homes and wait. They hoped that their circle would make the news the next day. The more attention a circle got, the better the fun. But recently, both men wondered if crop circle hoaxing was getting out of hand.

Doug Bower owned a picture framing shop when he met Dave Chorley in 1968. Both men were watercolor artists who loved practical jokes. The men became friends and would meet for a drink every Friday night at the Percy Hobbs pub, near Cheesefoot Head.

It was on one of those Friday nights in 1976 that Bower came up with the idea of crop circle hoaxing. It was a clear summer's night and the men decided to take a walk in the nearby wheat fields. They started talking about UFOs. Cheesefoot Head is not far from Warminster, where Arthur Shuttlewood claimed to have seen UFOs and crop circles in the 1970s. Both men had read Shuttlewood's books and remembered his reports of UFO "saucer nests." Bower had been in Australia at the time of the 1966 Tully UFO sighting and told Chorley about the saucer nests there, too.

Then Bower asked Chorley a question that forever changed the history of crop circles. "What do you think would happen if we put one over there? People would think a flying saucer had landed." Chorley liked the idea of fooling people: "Yeah, that sounds like a good idea," he said. The two then hatched a plan for their first circle.

The following Friday night, the men met again at the Percy Hobbs pub. This time they had a long iron bar with them. After waiting for the pub to close, the men walked to the wheat field at Cheesefoot Head. Getting on their hands and knees, the pair flattened a small round section of wheat with the bar. Then they went around the edge of that circle to make a bigger circle.

It was hard work, but before long they had made a thirty-foot-wide crop circle. Excited by their work, the men left the field, with Bower saying: "Look what we've done! This is sure to be spotted.

It won't be long before it's on the news." However, the next day, there was nothing. Nobody had seen the circle.

Bower and Chorley made several more circles that summer. Working under the light of the moon in fields of wheat felt both artistic and exciting. Bower would say to Chorley: "Do you realize that we are the only two people on this planet doing this and nobody in the world knows what's causing it?"

But after two years of hoaxing (enacting their well-planned pranks), the men's circles were still not getting noticed. Chorley wanted to give up. Bower, however, designed a new circle-making tool to make the job faster and easier. Bower's "stalk stomper" was a four-foot-long plank with a rope looped through a hole at either end. The hoaxers held the rope in their hands and pushed the plank down onto the crops with their feet.

Chorley agreed to continue, but only if they made circles where people would definitely see them.

In August 1980, the breakthrough came. Somebody had seen the three circles Bower and Chorley had made at the foot of the Westbury White Horse hill and called the local newspaper. "Mystery Circles—Return of the 'Thing'?" read the headline the next morning. Bower and Chorley were thrilled. They decided to keep hoaxing.

The men did have some near misses and close calls. One night, a farmer and his friends were rabbit hunting in the field next to where Bower and Chorley were creating a circle. The hoaxers had to lie flat on the ground until they passed.

Another time an object fell out of the sky and hit Chorley on the head! It turned out to be partly frozen human waste that had dropped from a high-flying plane overhead. The men quickly learned that hoaxing could be quite dirty work.

How Did They Do It?

Doug Bower always designed a crop circle on paper first. Then he and Dave Chorley would enter the field with the wooden stalk stomper, a ball of string, and a baseball cap.

To make a simple circle, Bower would hold one end of a piece of string and Chorley the other. Chorley would then move in a circle around Bower, flattening the crops with the stomper as he went. To make a bigger circle, Bower would let out more string, and Chorley would go around the outer edge of the existing circle. To make a straight line in the crops, Bower would use a sight, a device that helps focus a direct line, attached to his baseball cap. He aimed it at an object in the distance and flattened the crops as he walked toward it. The men walked along the field's tramlines near the thick crops to avoid making footprints.

By the time the hoaxers made the famous "quintuplet" formation in 1983, crop circles were making international news. The circles were also gaining the attention of the first crop circle researchers—Pat Delgado, Colin Andrews, and Terence Meaden. Bower and Chorley were amazed that the researchers suggested their quintuplet formation had been made by whirlwinds or energy fields. Bower said he had designed the quintuplet "to look like a four-legged spaceship had landed."

CHAPTER 7
Hoaxing Undercover

As interest in crop circles increased in the 1980s, so did the hoaxing of Bower and Chorley. The two men would lay out the circles on a Friday night and then join people viewing the circles the next day. Sometimes, there were traffic jams just to get to the circles. Bower and Chorley

would mix with the crowd and listen to their theories about what had created them. They often had to bite their lips to stop from laughing at the guesses.

Over time, Bower and Chorley became familiar faces at crop circle viewings and known to the researchers Pat Delgado, Colin Andrews, and Terence Meaden. Sometimes, they would even help the researchers measure the circles.

The researchers assumed Bower and Chorley were simply two local men who were interested in the circles—they never guessed that they were the ones creating them!

For Bower and Chorley, fooling the researchers with increasingly complicated formations became part of the game. But the researchers would simply adjust their theories to suit the new formations. Bower and Chorley designed the first pictogram to disprove Terence Meaden's whirlwind theory. After all, whirlwinds couldn't travel in straight lines. But Meaden then updated his theory to say that actually whirlwinds *could* move in straight lines. Pat Delgado and Colin Andrews said the pictograms were simply proof that some "superior intelligence" was urgently trying to make contact with humans. This amazed Bower and Chorley. "They called us 'superior intelligence' and this was the biggest laugh of all," Chorley later said.

The men had another reason for making the pictograms: new hoaxers had emerged. They were copying what Bower and Chorley had been doing, but with more complicated designs. After Bower and Chorley made the first ever pictogram, the other hoaxers made the Eastfield double pictogram that became so famous around the world. Bower and Chorley were now being outdone by their competitors. Some of them would become known to Bower and Chorley. Others, like the hoaxers at Operation Blackbird who had left the board game in their circle, remained anonymous. The competition aside, there were other reasons that being a crop circle hoaxer was becoming more difficult.

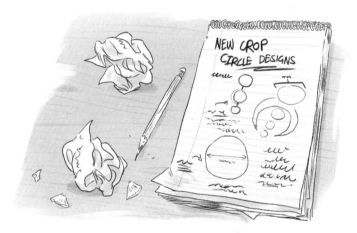

One night, Bower and Chorley were making a circle when a young crop circle tourist walked up on them. He had been meditating in a circle in a nearby field. He asked if the two men were pitching a tent and then left to let them continue with it. Another night, police officers drove past Bower and Chorley as they were getting into their car after completing a circle. It looked as though they had been caught red-handed, until Bower explained they had been recording bird calls. He did this in his spare time and had the equipment to prove it. Satisfied with the explanation, the police officers left them alone.

With so many people interested in crop circles, the chances of being caught were increasing. There were many people who wanted to be the first to solve the mystery of the circles. But also, the researchers were desperately trying to get evidence of a crop circle being made on film.

By the time Operation Blackbird began, Bower and Chorley were ready to end their careers as crop circle hoaxers. Although they watched the operation on the news, they weren't the hoaxers who made the circles at Westbury White Horse hill. However, Bower and Chorley's story was going to create even bigger news.

In September 1991, Bower and Chorley showed a journalist named Graham Brough from London's *Today* newspaper how they made a circle. Brough then called Pat Delgado to analyze this new crop circle. After investigating the circle,

Delgado announced: "This is without doubt the most wonderful moment of my research. No human could have done this."

Brough then brought out Doug Bower and Dave Chorley, who explained they had made the circle. In fact, they had been making the circles all along. Delgado looked devastated. "We have

Doug Bower and Dave Chorley explain their hoax to Pat Delgado

all been conned," he gasped. He said he and the other crop circle researchers would now look very foolish. Delgado then left to phone his fellow researcher, Colin Andrews.

The next day the newspaper revealed the hoax. Bower and Chorley assumed it would bring an end to the crop circle mystery that had riveted the world. But would it?

CHAPTER 8
Hoaxes Revealed

"MEN WHO CONNED THE WORLD" announced the front-page headline of *Today* newspaper on September 9, 1991. The article was several pages long, with photos of Doug Bower and Dave Chorley showing how they made the circles. It was an amazing story. Not only had the mystery of crop circles been solved, but the crop circle makers also were available for interviews. An international media frenzy followed.

Over the next few weeks, Bower and Chorley appeared on television talk shows in Italy, Germany, the Netherlands, and England. One English newspaper even filmed the pair walking around a crop circle in space suits as dry ice was sprayed around them. Now that crop circles had been exposed as hoaxes, the media could have fun with their creators.

The crop circle researchers were not amused, however. The *Today* story had indeed made them look foolish. Pat Delgado and Colin Andrews were the famous authors of *Circular Evidence*, who had claimed the circles were made by a supernatural superior intelligence. Terence Meaden insisted that at least some of the crop circles were made by whirlwinds. Many cereologists said it was impossible for every crop circle to have been made by hoaxers. Some even said Bower and Chorley were part of a government cover-up, or that their hoaxing story was simply to hide the fact that crop

circles were being made by visiting UFOs.

The media soon began to lose interest. For most of the public, the mystery was over. The following two summers in England were damp, and farmers harvested their crops early. They were also on the lookout for crop circle makers. Few circles emerged.

But in the summer of 1994, things began to change. Large, spectacular crop circle formations began to pop up all over southern England. Some formations were complicated mathematical patterns. Other formations were shaped like animals, such as spiders, scorpions, and beetles.

One of the best-known formations was the "Julia Set," named after a mathematical equation. This was a curved line of large and small circles near Stonehenge that looked like a centipede. A local pilot said he had flown over Stonehenge and then back one hour later, and the Julia Set had appeared within that time. It later emerged that three hoaxers, people who were still creating circles as pranks, had made the formation early that morning—the pilot had simply not noticed it on his first pass overhead.

The Julia Set

Once again, cereologists began claiming that the circles were being made by something other than humans. It was impossible, they said, for humans to make such complicated circles. Many hoaxers set out to prove them wrong. Around the rest of the world, crop circle formations were popping up in the Netherlands, Canada, and the United States.

Crop circle in the Netherlands, 2014

But nothing seemed to persuade believers in crop circles that humans were responsible. Several new investigations followed.

Yoshi-Hiko Ohtsuki

Terence Meaden still insisted that some of the circles were made by his Plasma Vortex Theory. A Japanese professor of plasma physics, Yoshi-Hiko Ohtsuki, investigated this theory. He found that a plasma could, indeed, form a simple crop circle, but not a pictogram with straight lines and complicated patterns.

However, balls of light and crop circles continued to be a mystery. Many insisted that the lights were the UFOs making the circles.

Then, one day in 1996, that evidence seemed to surface. Crop circle enthusiast John Wheyleigh had been up early on August 11 with his video camera. He claimed that suddenly, four floating balls of light appeared over a field of wheat. The balls swooped down, and the wheat was flattened into a snowflake formation. Then the balls sped away. The whole video lasted twelve seconds.

The video was shown to an excited crowd at the Barge Inn pub, at Alton Barnes, Wiltshire. This was a popular meeting place for cereologists.

Bruce Logan

Soon, the footage was being screened around the world. Hollywood special effects expert Bruce Logan thought it was genuine. "Only a handful of people in the world would be capable of such work. I think it's extremely unlikely this is not genuine," Logan said.

Logan, however, was wrong. The video had been made by a team of three hoaxers. They had first made the circle formation and then superimposed the balls of light using special-effects software. The cameraman, as it turned out, also worked for a digital film studio. Once again, crop circle believers had been fooled.

Signs (2002)

Directed by M. Night Shyamalan, *Signs* is the best-known movie that links crop circles with UFOs. It tells the story of an American farmer who finds crop circle formations in his cornfield. He assumes they are the work of hoaxers, but many other circles suddenly start appearing all over the world. It turns out that the crop circles—along

with the strange hovering lights that surround them—are a navigational tool for alien life forms who have arrived to invade Earth. The crop circles had been "signs" of their arrival.

CHAPTER 9
Crop Circles Today

After the proven crop circle hoaxes of the '90s, many expected them to stop appearing. But they showed up not only in southern England, but also all over the world. The nature of the circles, however, was changing.

In 2014, a crop circle that looked like a computer chip appeared in a barley field in Chualar, California. Hundreds flocked to see it. Some said other, perhaps alien, life forms had made it. One visitor asked the farmer not to mow the circle so others could "go in and experience the energy." Later, it emerged that hoaxers had made the circle to advertise a new computer chip. The circle had been a publicity stunt.

Crop circle–like art has been used by businesses ever since to advertise Papa John's pizza, the *South Park* television show, the Olympic Games, and even candidates for the 2020 American presidential election. Professionals are hired to create this art.

One such artist, Stan Herd, created giant portraits of Democratic party presidential candidate Joe Biden and his running mate, Kamala Harris, in a field in Douglas County, Kansas. The portraits measured around two acres across and took days for Herd and his eight helpers to complete. Herd was not paid to do the art, but instead raised money from local donors to complete it.

Back in Wiltshire, England, tourists today

pay for crop circle tours and visit the Crop Circle Exhibition and Information Centre, where T-shirts and books are available. Crop circles continue to be good for business.

In 2020, dozens of large crop circles appeared in English crop fields. These were formations of snowflakes, stars, and even the imagined head of an extraterrestrial. Crop circle tour companies arrange with the farmers to visit new field art. But they never say what or who created them.

For many visitors, the appeal still remains in the mystery of how they came to be.

Cereologists continue to insist crop circles are made by supernatural forces, despite all of the hoaxing evidence. They say eyewitness accounts of UFOs, balls of light, and field crops being flattened before people's eyes prove this. The 1966 crop circles in Tully, Australia, are a good example. Scientists, however, say that eyewitness accounts do not provide solid evidence. Perhaps we will never know why or how the crop circles appeared in Tully.

In the search for truth, who do we believe? Hundreds of years ago, fairies and baskets from the sky may have seemed likely explanations for crop circles. Today, we look to science for rational explanations. Often, there is a simple, unexciting answer. But for many it is more exciting to believe in a mystery than a mere human prank.

Timeline of Crop Circles

1678 — *Mowing Devil* pamphlet shows an early English crop circle

1686 — Professor Robert Plot investigates circular "fairy rings"

1880 — Scientist John Rand Capron suggests whirlwinds make crop circles

1964 — A farmer's son reports a UFO and crop circle in Oregon

1966 — UFO "saucer nests" are reported in Tully, Australia

1972 — English journalist Arthur Shuttlewood reports seeing a crop circle being formed

1976 — Doug Bower and Dave Chorley begin making crop circles

1980 — Three crop circles are discovered below the Westbury White Horse, England

1983 — First "quintuplet" crop circle appears

1989 — Over three hundred crop circles appear in southern England

1990 — Operation Blackbird aims to capture a crop circle being made

1991 — Doug Bower and Dave Chorley are revealed as crop circle hoaxers

1994 — Complicated mathematical crop circle formations appear

2002 — The movie *Signs* is released

2020 — Crop circle art is used to advertise some of the 2020 American presidential candidates

Timeline of the World

1678 — Elena Cornaro becomes the first woman to receive a university degree: a degree in philosophy from Padua University in Italy

1787 — The United States Constitution is signed in Philadelphia

1861 — American Civil War begins

1945 — World War II ends when Japan surrenders to the United States

1952 — The United States Air Force launches Project Blue Book to record and study UFO sightings

1957 — The Soviet Union launches the first satellite into space

1969 — American Neil Armstrong becomes the first man on the moon

1975 — The Vietnam War ends

1982 — The movie *E.T. the Extra-Terrestrial*, about a visiting extraterrestrial, is released

1990 — The Hubble Space Telescope is launched into space to take photos of the universe

1994 — Apartheid ends in South Africa

2008 — Worldwide Great Recession begins

2011 — World population reaches seven billion people

2020 — Joe Biden is elected the forty-sixth president of the United States

Bibliography

*Books for young readers

Anderhub, Werner, and Hans Peter Roth. *Crop Circles: Exploring the Designs & Mysteries*. New York: Sterling Publishing, 2002.

Delgado, Pat, and Colin Andrews. *Circular Evidence*. London, UK: Bloomsbury Publishing Limited, 1989.

Glickman, Michael. *Crop Circles: The Bones of God*. Berkeley, CA: Frog Books, 2009.

Haselhoff, Eltjo. *The Deepening Complexity of Crop Circles*. Berkeley, CA: Frog Books, 2001.

Irving, Rob, John Lundberg, and Mark Pilkington. *The Field Guide: The Art, History and Philosophy of Crop Circle Making*. London, UK: Strange Attractor Press, 2006.

*Oxlade, Chris. *The Mystery of Crop Circles*. Chicago: Heinemann Library, 2001.

Sagan, Carl. *The Demon-Haunted World*. New York: Ballantine Books, 1996.

Schnabel, Jim. *Round in Circles: Poltergeists, Pranksters, and the Secret Society of the Cropwatchers*. New York: Prometheus Books, 1994.

Silva, Freddy. *Secrets in the Fields: The Science and Mysticism of Crop Circles*. Newburyport, MA: Hampton Roads, 2002.

Wilson, Terry. *The Secret History of Crop Circles: Recording the Phenomenon in Days of Old*. Paignton, UK: The Center for Crop Circle Studies, 1998.